ANIMAL ALLEGORIES

A Collection of Bas Reliefs Portraying Human/Animal Relationships

Second Edition

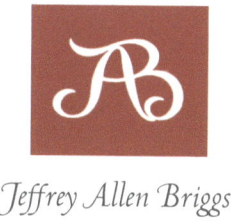

Jeffrey Allen Briggs

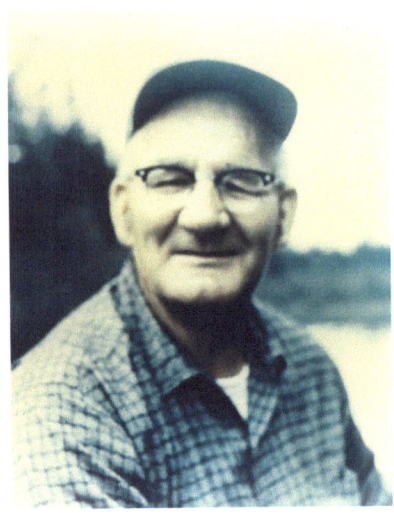

Dedicated to Charles Judson Briggs

Born, April 17, 1899
Dubois, Pennsylvania
Died, December 22, 1967
Dover-Foxcroft, Maine

Woodsman, Naturalist, Farmer, and Nature Guide

ANIMAL ALLEGORIES

I have always believed that art should contribute to the moral and spiritual elevation and social betterment of its audience. The series of bas reliefs in this book highlight themes and questions related to humankind's relationship to animals. Of particular concern to me is the loss of animal species due to our continuing destruction of the environment. The future course of the Earth's biosphere will be determined by our actions and as a fellow human and artist, I seek to contribute to the decades-long effort to make people aware of the effects of our choices on the environment and the animals around us.

I believe the way that we treat animals reflects on our ability to become true stewards of the earth. The intention of this series of wall reliefs is to make the viewer more conscious of the ethical and psychological attitudes he or she may have inherited. As an artist, I want to use the strength of the pictorial image to raise awareness of the paradoxical attitudes we hold toward animal. My hope is that the awareness of these paradoxes will advance the changes necessary for us to better manage the earth's resources.

You may look at some of these works and see no obvious connections to my statements on the environment. My purpose in the work is not to illustrate the subject matter but create images that help the viewer better understand the deep seated assumptions about what we consider acceptable treatment of animals. Hammering home a particular message is not my intention. I think this has already happened too much within the debate on the environment. I would rather have the viewer return to look again and question where these assumptions come from. In my mind, in order to achieve this, the work has to be subtle and at the same time intriguing and unsettling. I want the viewer to question what I am saying in the work as well as what he or she thinks about the subject of the work.

Jeffrey A. Briggs, Newburyport, MA

AFFINITY

Animal Kinship

There is an emotional attraction between us and other mammals. The attraction, represented by the connecting chain in this work, is that voluntary drawing together of kinship with animals. Maybe it is the inherent similarity between us. After all, we are all blood, bone and beating heart. We mammals sleep, eat and breathe air. We are protected by our skins but only separated from one another by those skins.

Notice that the chain has a manacle at the human end and a neck collar at the other, similar to a dog leash. They are bound together in an unequal relationship. What is it that makes us feel we must be the master in the human/animal relationship?

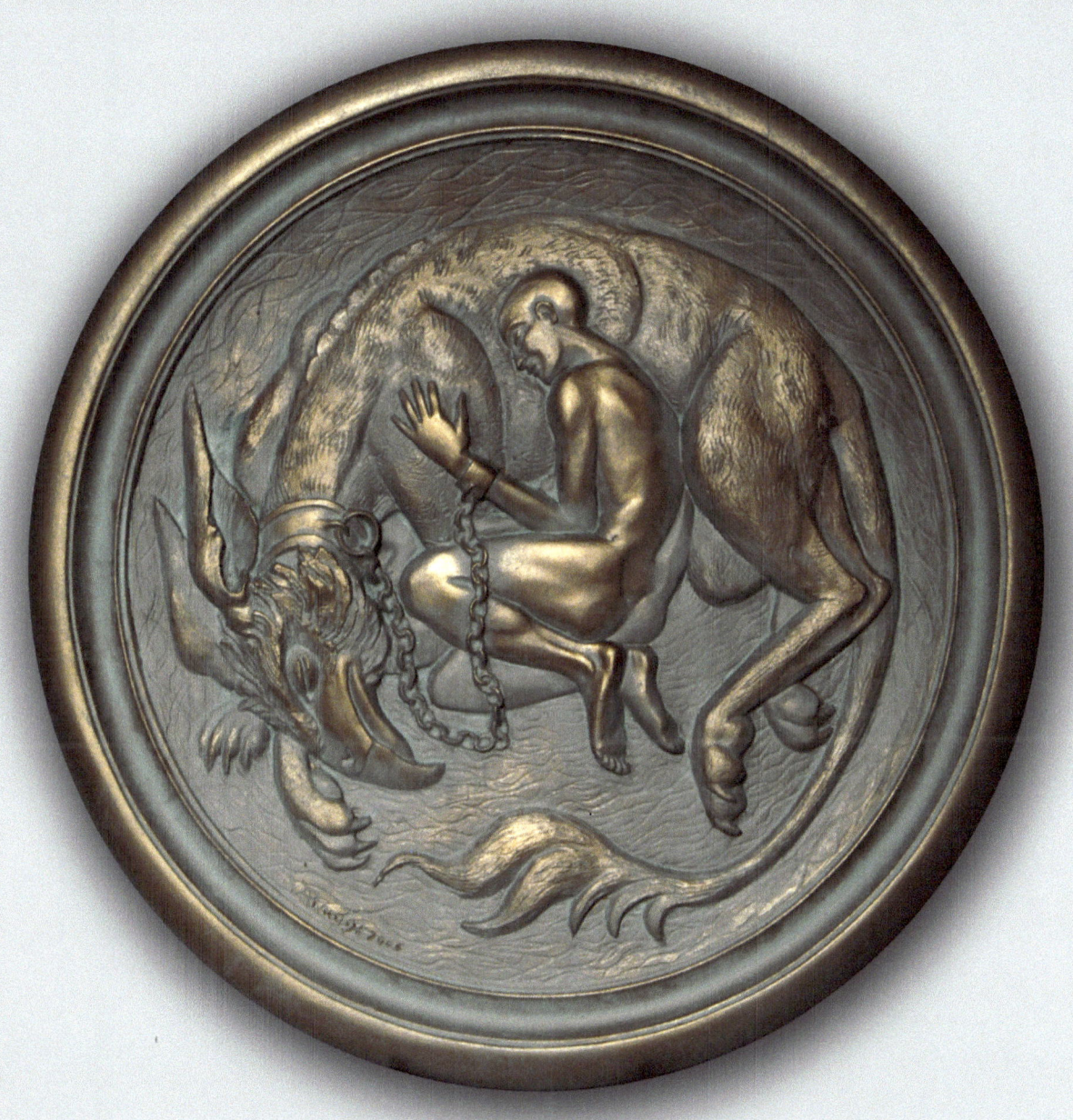

BABIRUSA

Animal love

Zoophilism is a psychological description of people who extremely love animals. Another clinical definition is someone who is sexually/romantically attracted to nonhuman animals. The babirusa with the small child is used to show that humans are capable of loving almost any animal, no matter how awful it may look or feel.

The babirusa is an East Indian swine. It has a rough, greyish, almost hairless hide and lives in the dense jungle, foraging for roots in rivers and swamps. It develops big, dangerous looking teeth or tusks yet is a docile, retiring, night hunting animal. I have used the perilous look of the babirusa as an example of our amazing ability to love any animal.

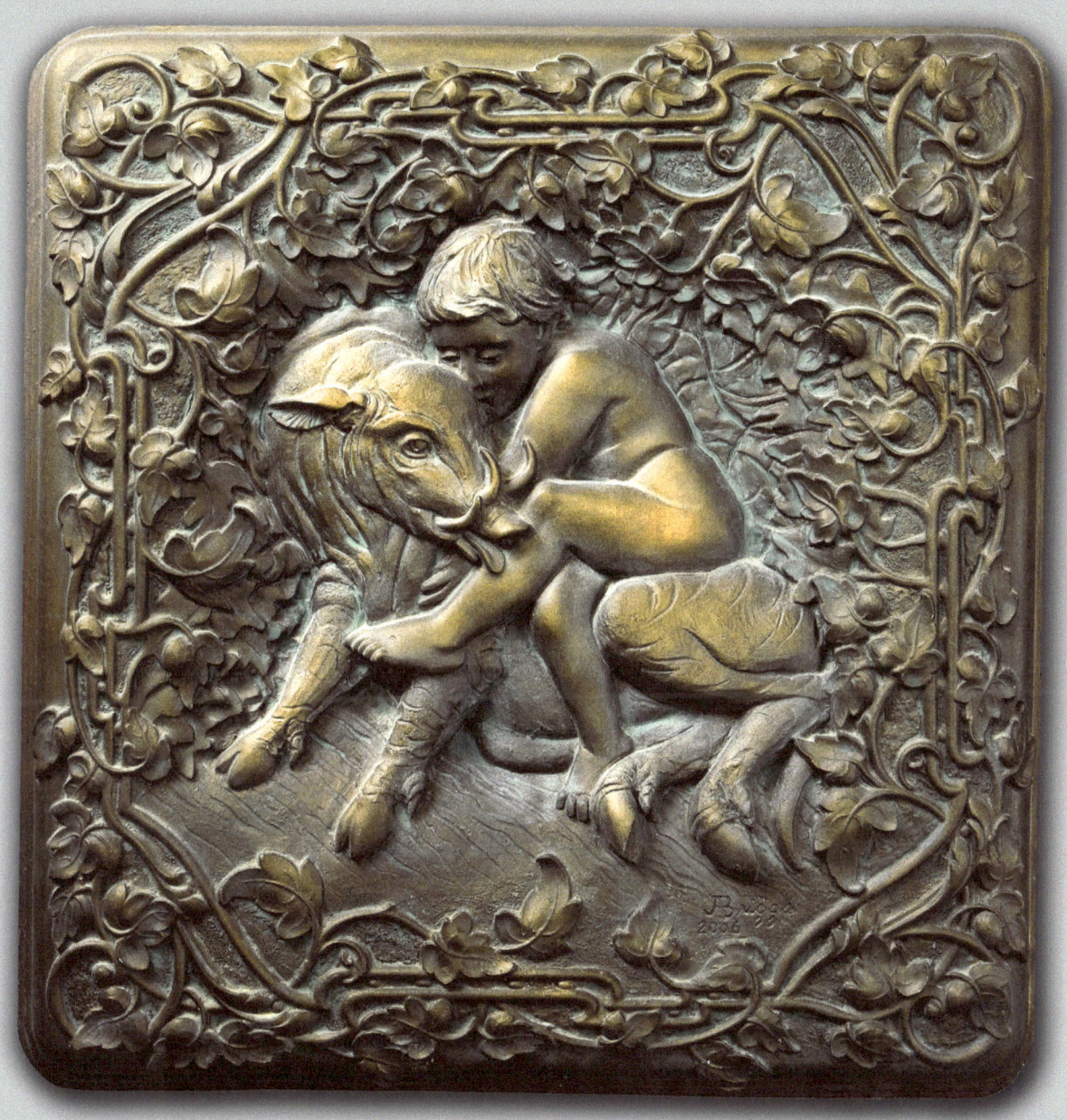

Behemoth

Animal Exploitation

Controlling exotic animals has always been a way to show off wealth and secure stature for us humans. From King Wen's menagerie in 1100 B.C. China to P. T. Barnum's 1850 "museum" in the U.S., animals on display—whether as show animals or in present day zoos—has been a form of exploitation. In the glorified exploits of the hunter adventurers of the 18th and 19th centuries to the story of King Kong, the more dangerous the animal the more dramatic the mastery over them. Maybe the need to see a powerful animal seized and contained placates some inner primordial need of ours.

Behemoth is a curious word for me. It is a powerful grass-eating animal with "limbs like bars of iron" (Job 40:10). I use it here to mean an enormous unidentified animal.

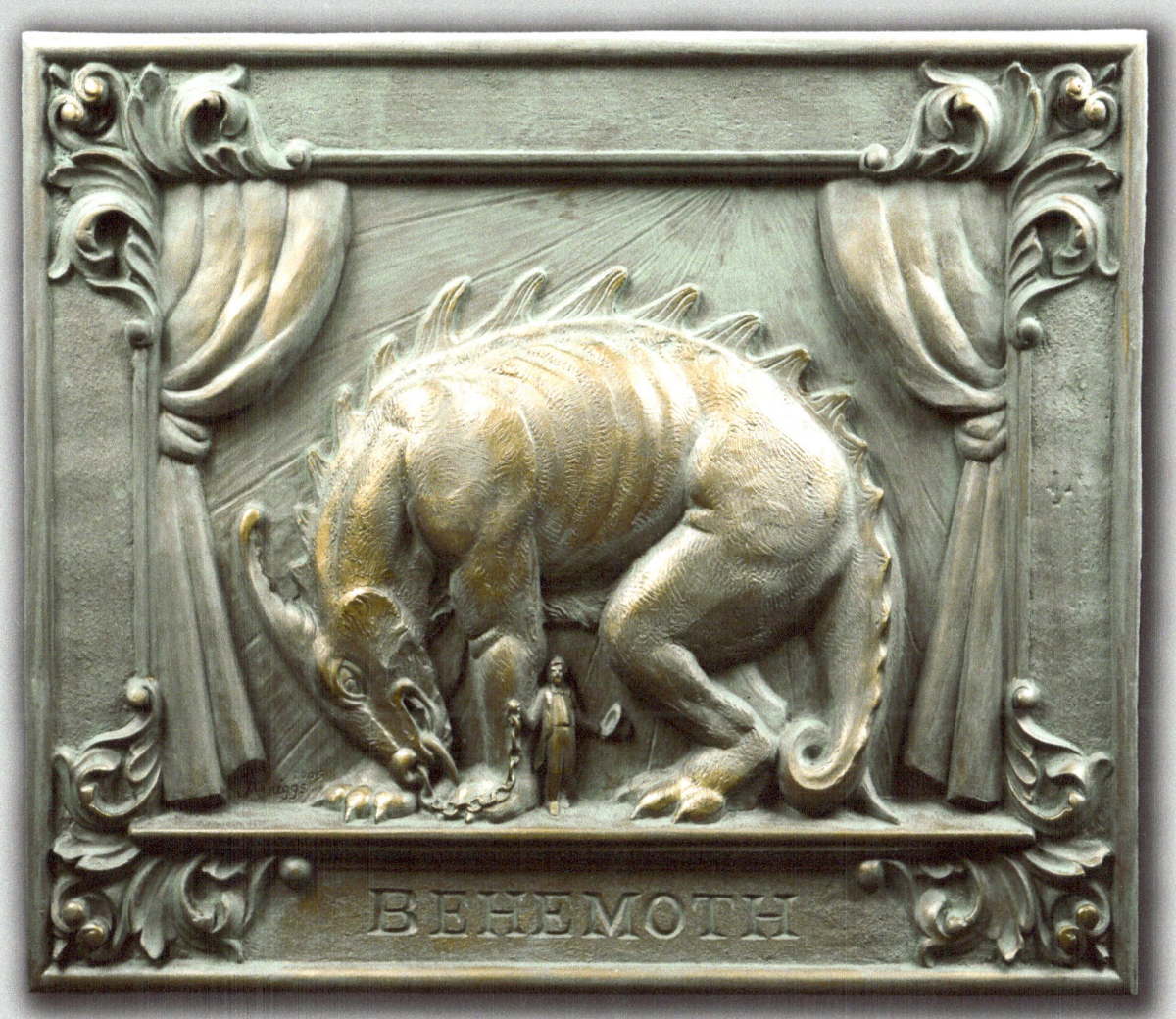

BEHEMOTH

DEMIGOD

Worshiping Animals

I found this subject difficult to portray. Animal worship is not commonly found in modern society. I hope that adding the title Demigod to the work would aid the viewer in placing the subject in context. Demigod is an interesting word: a half god, one with godlike attributes. In today's Western culture, we interpret the word demigod to mean an unworthy religion or false belief and I have used it in the same way here in this work.

From our earliest beginnings animals showed up in our myths and folklore as gods and omens. Animism, the belief that soul and spirit resides in every object, is one of the oldest of human spiritual beliefs. Ancient hunting people performed ceremonies—maybe in the hope of placating powerful predators by granting them sacred status. This worship by ancient societies eventually became rationalized and abstract. The sacred power of a deity was believed to be manifested in an animal and was regarded as an incarnation of the deity. For example, the bull frequently represents fertility deities. In modern societies where animals take on the role of totems or emblems, there are taboos against people eating or killing certain animals. To these totem groups the believer identifies with the animal and becomes a relative or guardian of the animal. Some forms of Hinduism hold these beliefs.

Animal symbolism in religion has been used to represent certain qualities of certain animal species, for example the wisdom of the owl. There are remainders of this symbolism in our daily life when we name a car, Cougar or sports team the Bears.

This piece is to remind us that we continue to view animals in spiritual ways even in our modern technical world.

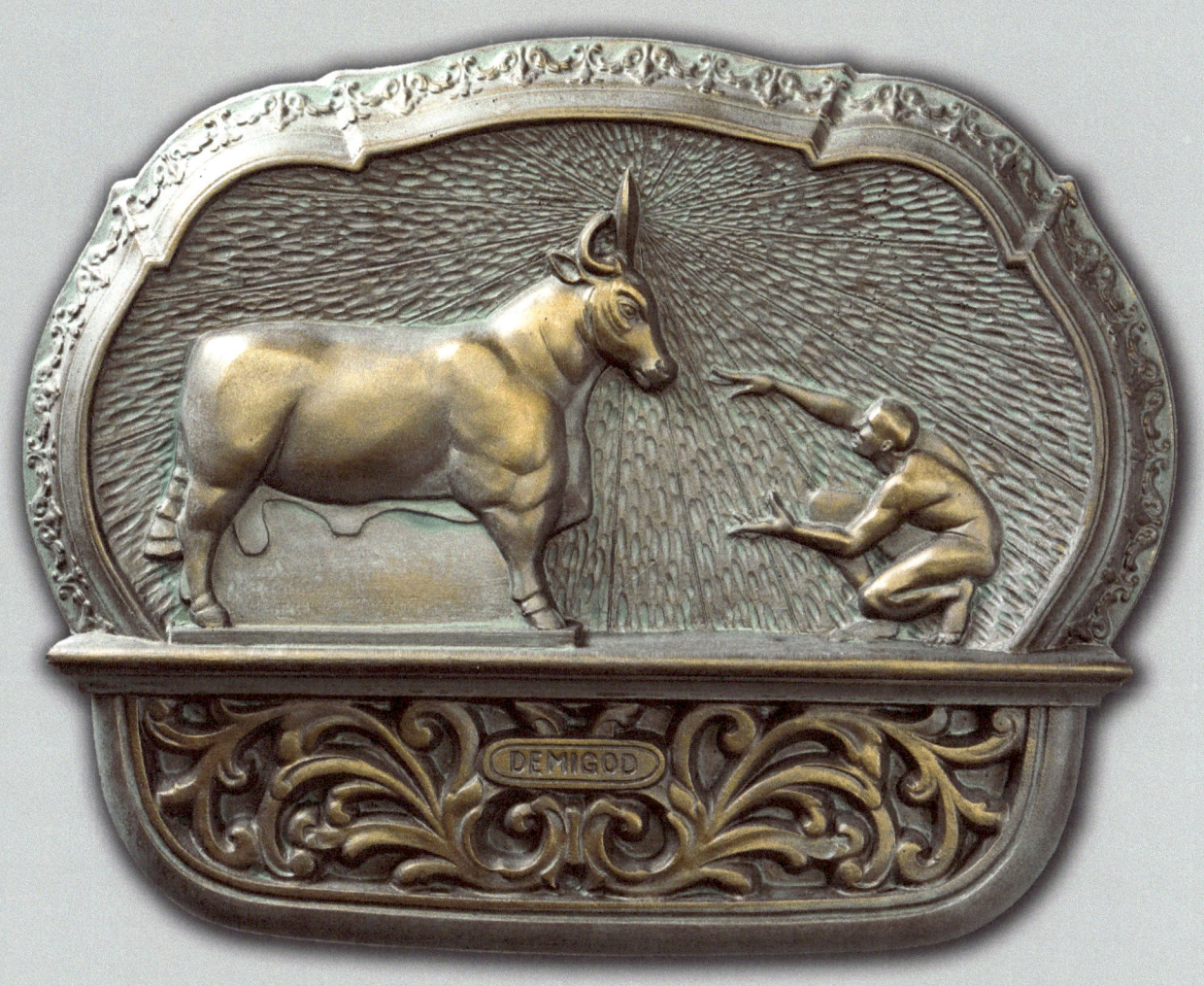

Hyena

Animal Conservation

Animal conservation has many contradictory facets. Some animals we selectively breed for food, while letting their original ancestral livestock almost disappear. With other animals we protect their territorial environments for sustainable exploitation. We are breeding a few animals in captivity to keep them from extinction, and in the meantime, we are making their habitats inhospitable. We go to great lengths to save some endangered animals while driving thousands of others into extinction. Saving and at the same time destroying is the subject of this piece.

In this work, the human is giving water to the animal. The human has a bow over his shoulder. There is an arrow in the back of the animal. The saving (the water) and the destroying (the arrow) becomes the paradox of the relationship. Maybe what we are really doing in conservation is deciding which creature we will keep on earth with us.

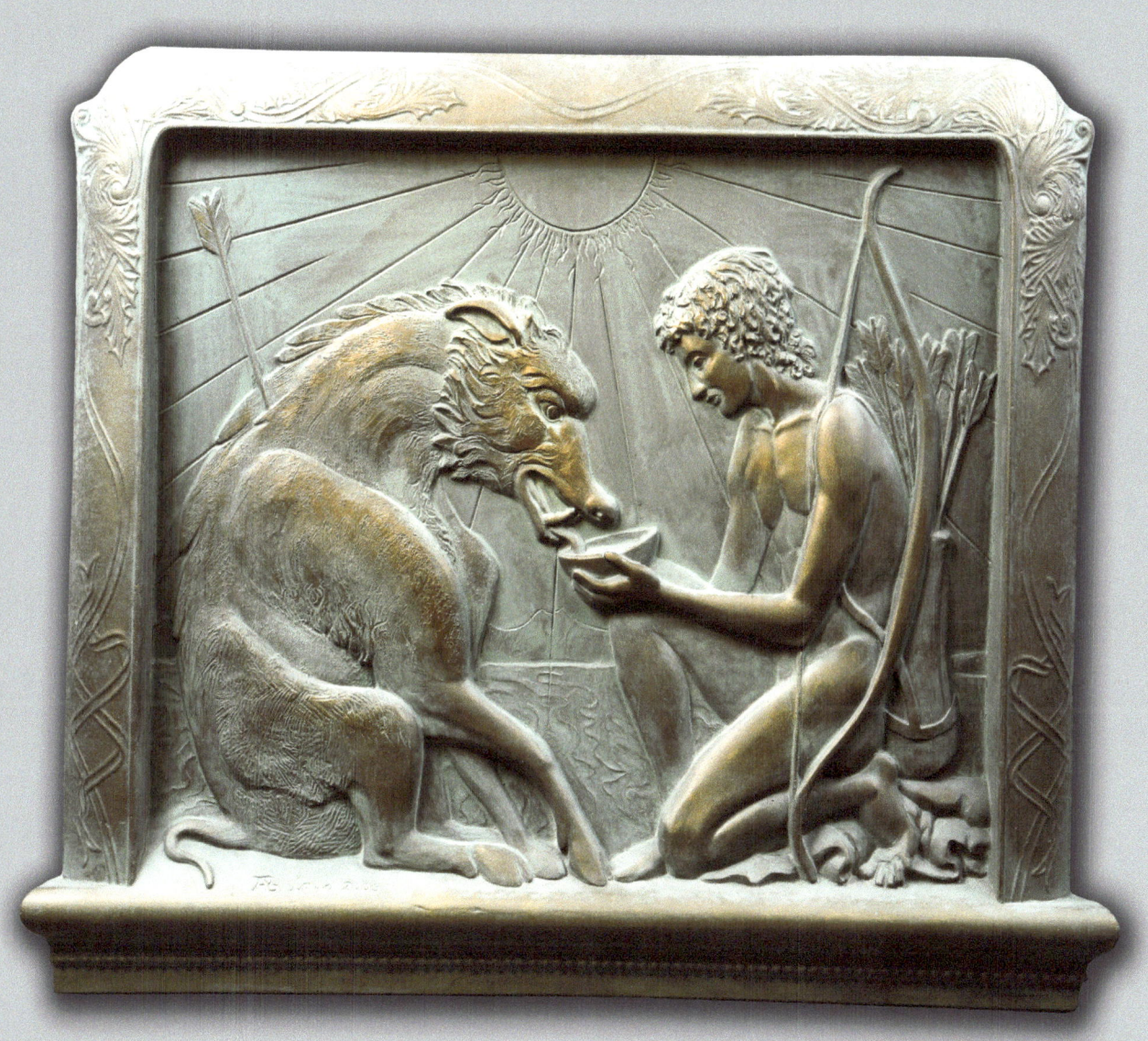

Kiwi

Animal Extinction

It is estimated that by the end of the 21st century, two thirds of all the animals on the planet will be extinct. Human actions are the main source of this sweeping extinction. Paradoxically we use our awesome creative capabilities—thanks to large, highly developed brains, dexterous fingers with opposing thumbs that give us the means to craft nearly anything in our dominance and degradation of the earth.

In this work, the man has made a disguise from an elk's skin, using deception to chase the quarry (the Kiwi) into his net. The flightless Kiwi is no longer abundant and I have used it to express how helpless animals are compared to ingenious humans. The work is meant to ask the question why is it that human beings can use these advanced skills merely to use the planet's resources. Why can't we use this ability to begin working for a healthy earth? We are an integral part of the planet but continue to view ourselves as something separate. Just as the elk's skin is a deception to the Kiwi, it is also a delusion to the human masking himself from the rest of the earth.

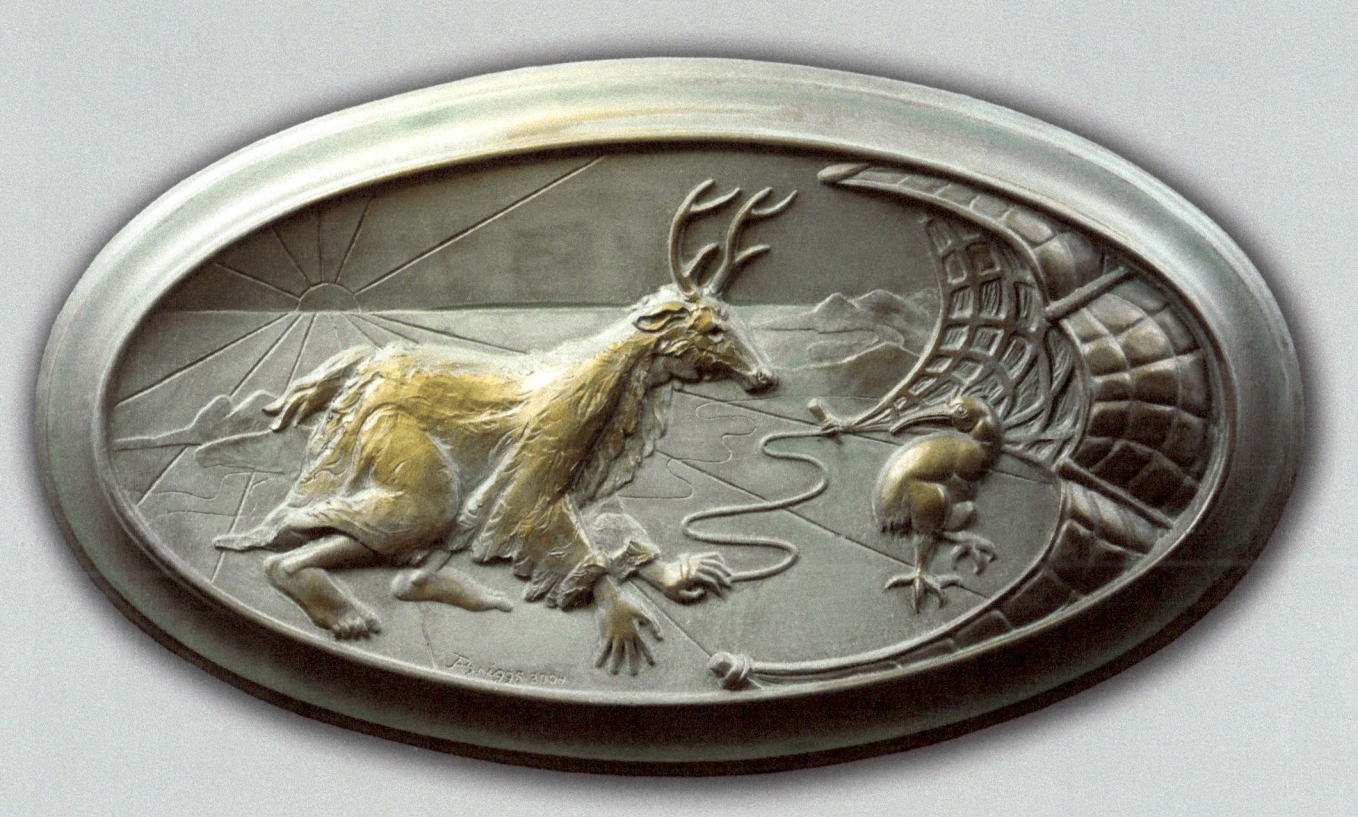

13

Knossos

Humans and Animals at Play

This work harkens back to the bull dancer of the ancient Minoan civilization in Greece. The dancer/jumper plays with the bull by somersaulting over its back. It was an acrobatic stunt believed to be part of a Minotaur religious celebration that took place in the Minoan capital of Knossos.

Animals and humans share a love of fun and evidence of humans playing with other animals exists throughout history.

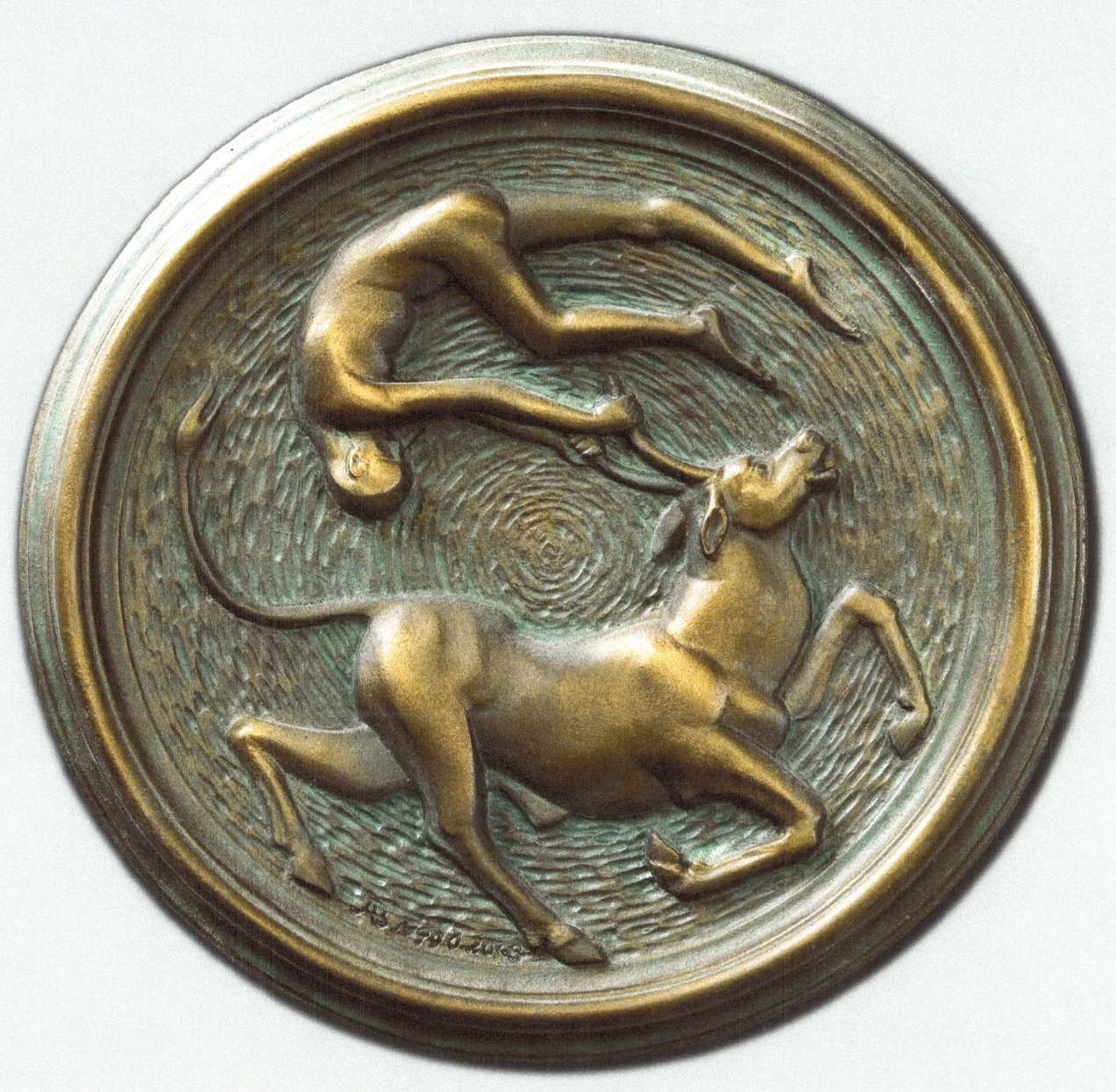

NEREID

The Mythology of Animals

The dolphin is the kindly servant of antiquity, the rescuer of drowning people, the talisman against fires, the emblem of success in the arts, a messenger of good fortune and a mascot of safe travel. These are just a few of the qualities that have been attributed to the dolphin in human history. People 's fascination with and connection to dolphins have mythologized them into spiritual creatures. Researchers have found that dolphins talk back-and-forth to each other for hours on end. Because they are predators of the sea, as we are of the land, and because of their social fabric they are referred to as "the humans of the sea". I find it paradoxical in the face of our advanced scientific knowledge of them we continue to mythologize them even today.

Of course, dolphins are not the only animals that humans have used in mythology. In this piece they represent the subject matter in general.

A Nereid is from Greek mythology. She is the beneficial sea nymph, and daughter of the sea god Poseidon. She completes the mythical theme of this work of art.

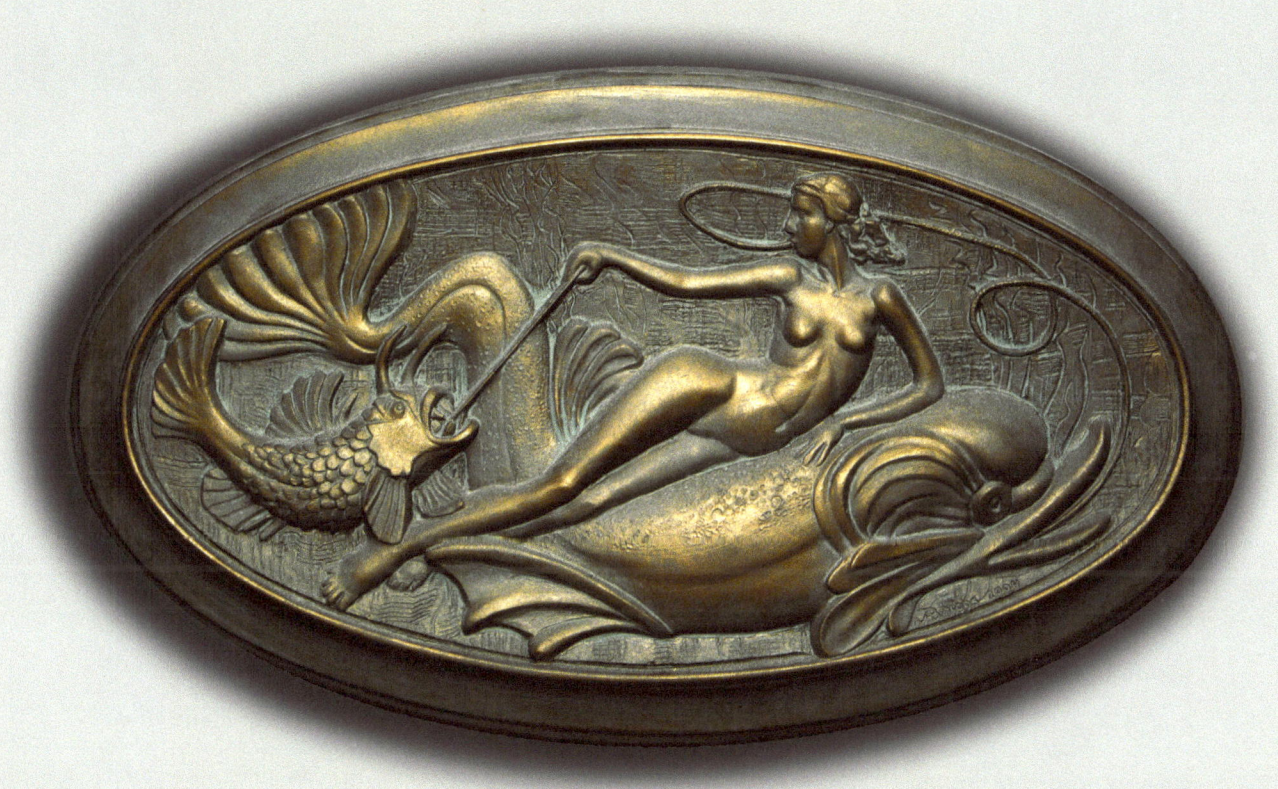

17

Pegasus

Dominance

With our large brains and useful hands humans have been able to dominate nearly all other animals. We exert control over even the greatest of them, by seizing, restraining and forcibly confining them.

This work expresses that moment when humans drive the spirit of free will from other fellow animals. Maybe our motive is to tame, domesticate, breed, to feed our ever mushrooming populations or maybe our reason for controlling is simply to satisfy our need for a pet.

Pegasus's soaring flight in Greek antiquity was interpreted as an allegory of the soul's immortality. If one interprets the soul as the intangible spiritual nature of humankind, why should it not follow that other animals have souls too. Maybe the proof of this is that for many animals we wish to dominate we must capture, restrain and confine each and every one. We drive the spirit away to have it return anew with each animal.

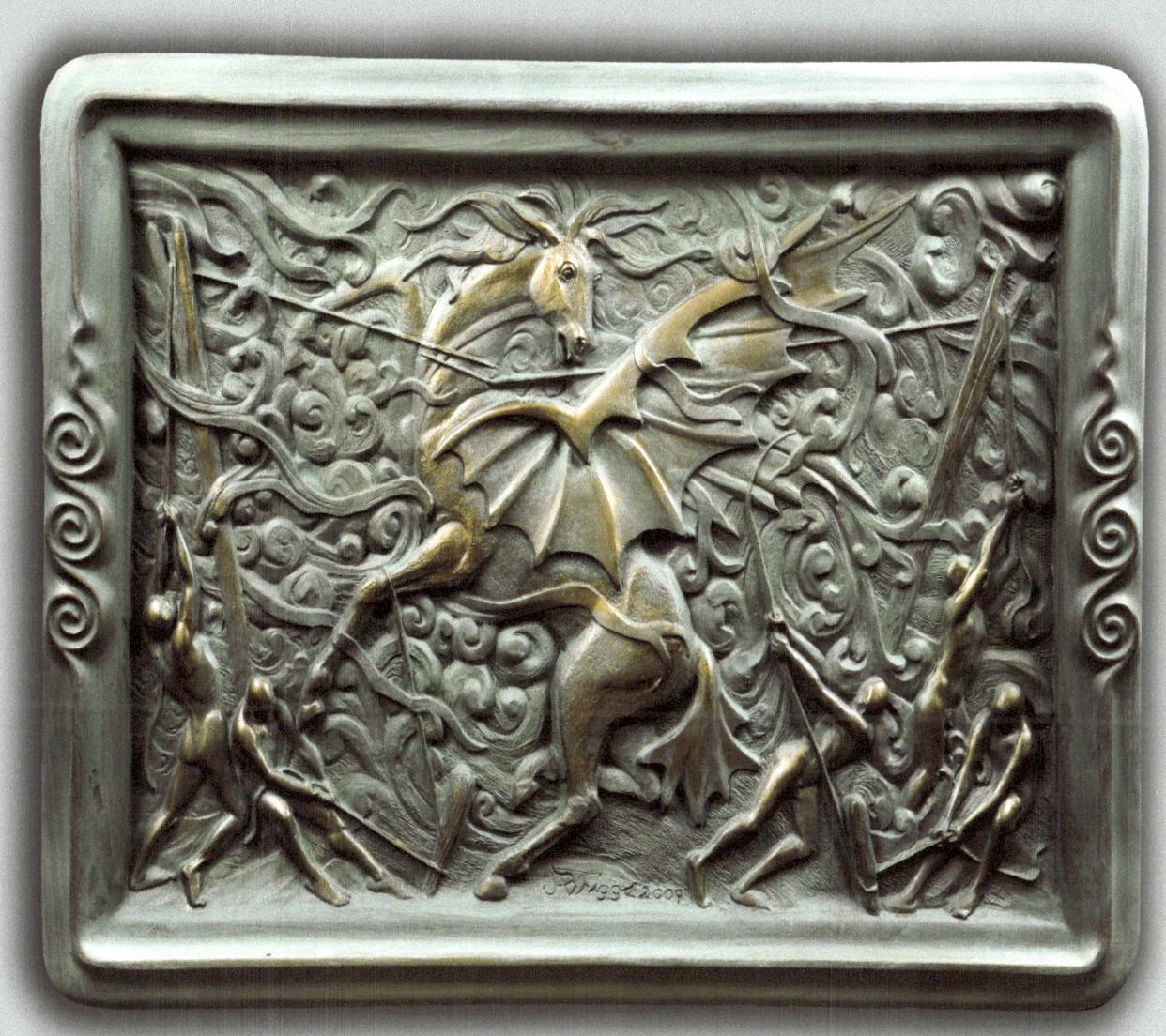

Predator

Who is the Monster?

Large predators inspire awe and humble us even in this day and age. Maybe they remind us of our limitations or perhaps they threaten our image as masters of the planet in which we are the predators but rarely the prey. The bold predator has paid dearly by our wrath as we have pushed many of them into extinction. Some researchers say that all free-ranging predators will disappear by 2050. The mythic vision of predators has played an important role in shaping our own species. In contemporary times, we find roles for predators within our emotional universe in movies and our daily news. Picture a future when big predators cease to exist, they recede from memory and people will find it hard to imagine what these animals meant to us. At that point, do we replace these big predators as the terrible monsters?

This work is inspired by the painting, *The Sleeping Gypsy* by Henri Rousseau.

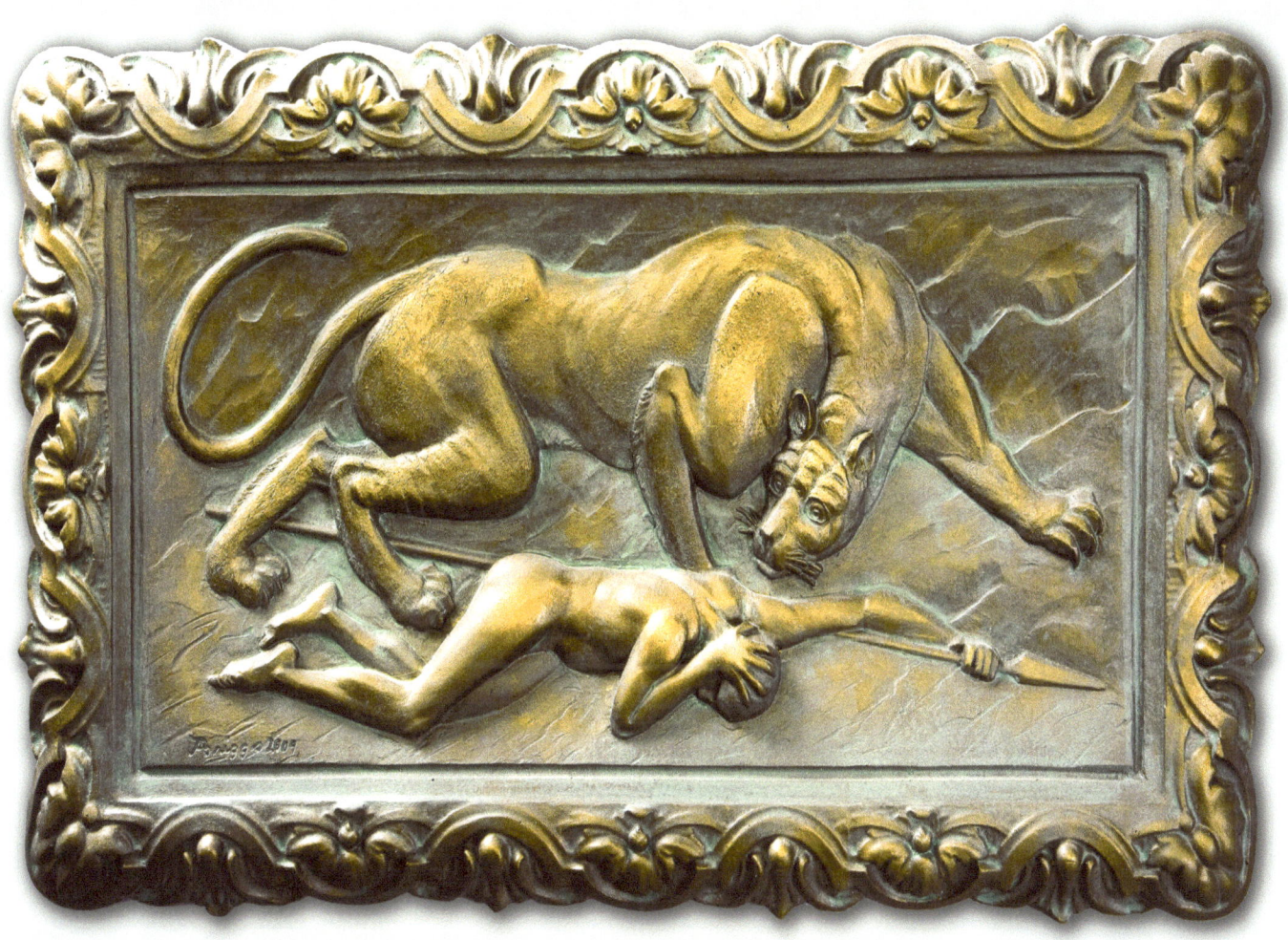

Primordial Hunt

Hunting

While hunting, I experienced strong feelings I didn't know I possessed. I felt a total consciousness of the environment around me. These intensified sights, sounds, smells, and feelings coupled with the ability to hunt and kill brought out a predatory instinct that humans have felt since prehistory.

In this work, I have tried to capture the moment when the hunter coalesces with the inner animal self in the chase of the quarry. I have used the forest god Pan, half human half animal, to express this. In mythology, the god Pan, exuded menace and triggered panic in the forest. The rabbit is the expression of that danger. Dogs have been a partner with humans in the chase since around 12,000 BC. Some paleozoologists theorize that dogs taught humans better ways to hunt.

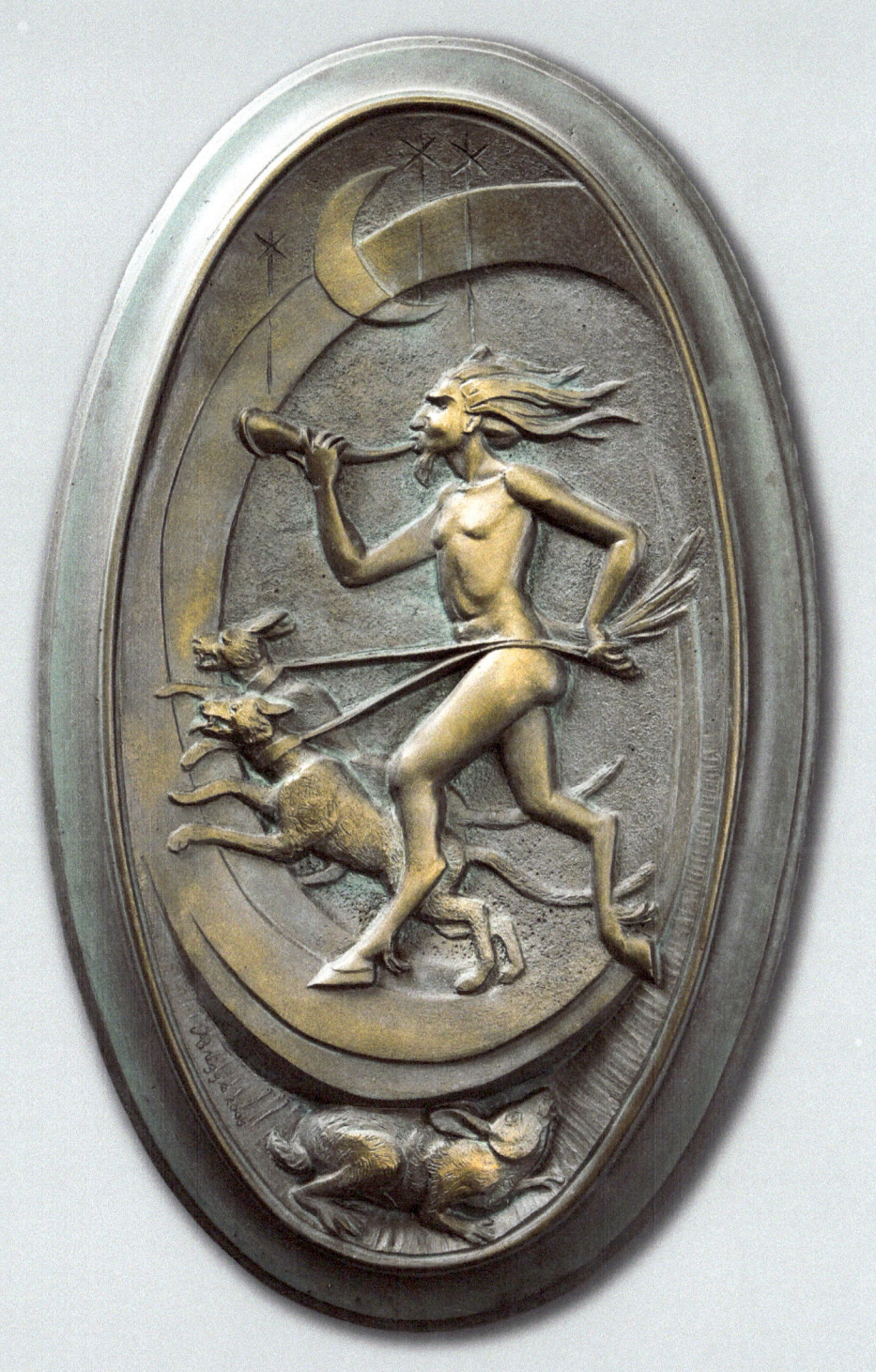

23

STANDARD OF PERFECTION

Animal Breeding

Animal breeding is defined as, "the controlled propagation of domestic animals to improve qualities desirable by man." Humans have been tinkering with many animal species, and especially cows, since Neolithic times, around 10,000 BC. The cow is certainly one of the most successfully domesticated animals. Beginning in the 18th century the practice of judging "utility breeds" on their physical structure and conformity with breed standards was instituted to improve the cow. Traits considered desirable are easy production, attachment of the udder to the body, record of high milk production, and conformation standards. The only way an animal makes this superior, desirable ranking is to be docile, submissive, cheap to feed, immune to diseases, grow rapidly and breed well in captivity. Without man's continuous care and solicitude the dairy cow could not exist. We have engineered a dependent creature: artificially inseminated and D.N.A. selected breeding creations has created the "purebred" standard. The scientific research on better ways of raising healthy livestock has led to new developments including "cloned replicas" and "chimeras" (mixing of cells to create improved body parts). These are the new advancements in the Standard of Perfection—a chilling term I learned from a television program on judging dairy cows.

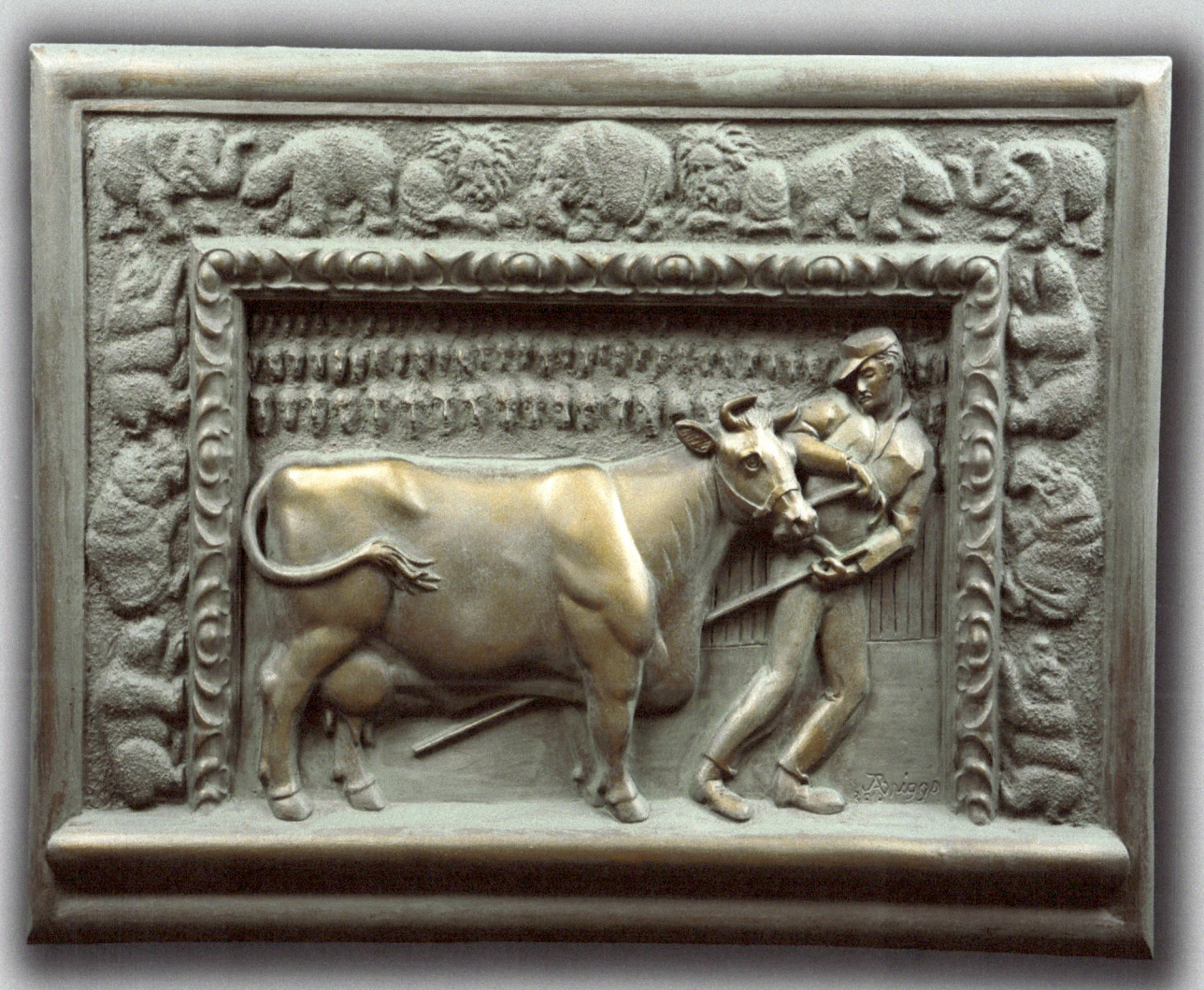

Taxonomy

Classification of Animals

Taxonomy is the process of classifying animals, plants, species, genera and kingdoms. People have taken a scientific approach to identifying living things. This sorting of nature makes it easier to discuss and of course to manage. It is ironic that the very moment humans are learning more and more about our natural world, we are driving greater numbers of animals into extinction.

I have used the scholarly image of Saint Jerome to represent humankind. He is holding a caliper up to the wing. This is a method that I saw in a film used to tell the age of birds. I used the cow in this piece because it is one of the first domesticated animals, presumably about 10,000 years ago. This creature is the most repeatedly, independently domesticated animal of mankind. We have had a long relationship with the cow species.

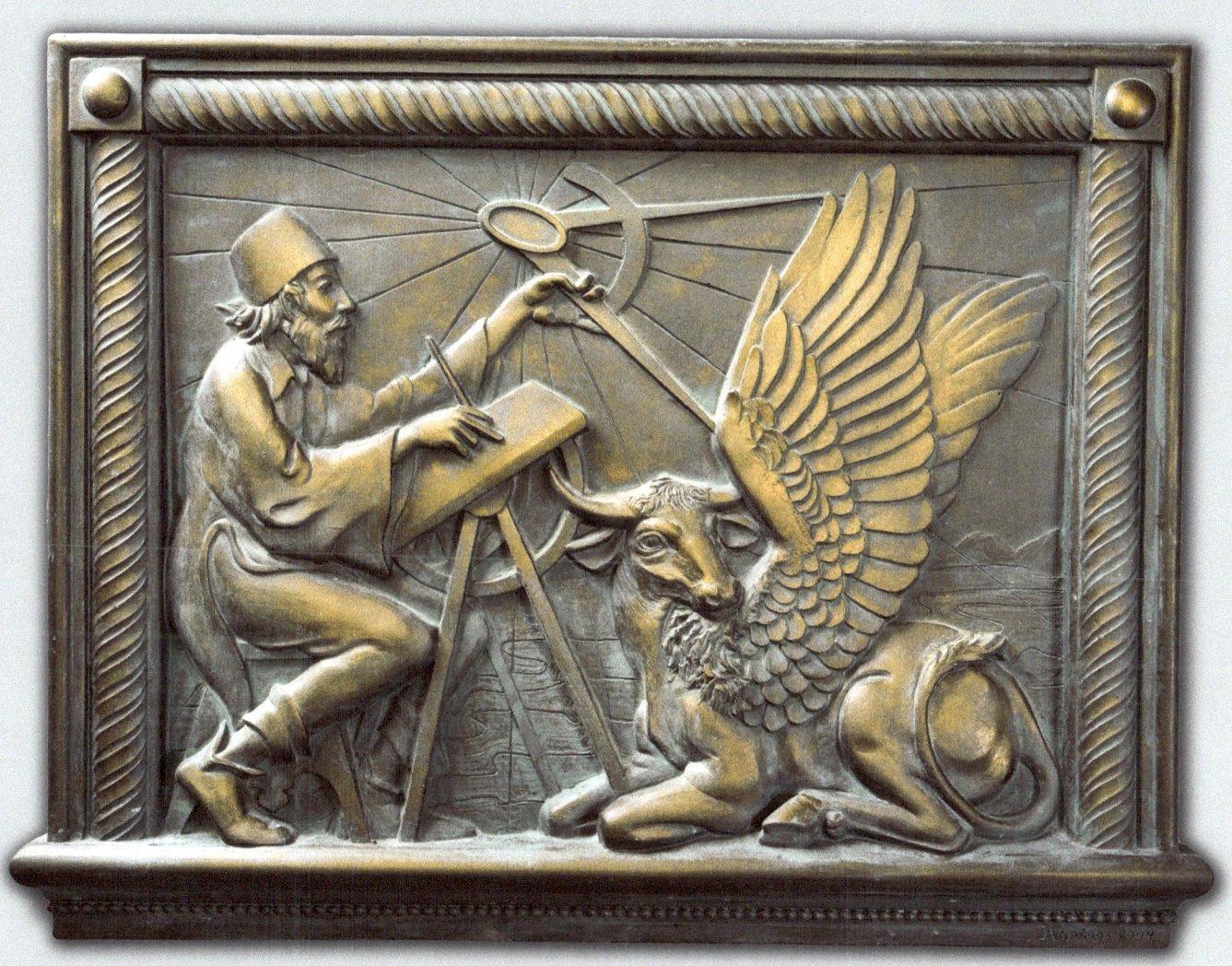

The Messenger

Communicating with Animals

Our efforts to communicate with other animals has been an eternal quest. Many of us have experienced the belief that we can understand what a fellow mammal is communicating to us. But in reality the void between them and us seems never truly bridged.

This work is my attempt to imagine that moment when this void is crossed. I have selected the symbol of the winged lion of Saint Mark the apostle as the animal world's messenger. The winged lion is a motif used to represent a leader or advocate of a cause. The scene depicts the moment when the advocate has come before the human. Finally the time has come when animals share thoughts with us. After all they share with us the same characteristics from which love, terror, grief, compassion and shame spring from. But, the Messenger's silence is as quiet as the material that this work of art is made of. Perhaps this is because the winged lion is also used as a motif for the guardian of gates and temples.

Animal intelligence springs from a different perception and understanding of the world than our own. Perhaps the void between man and animals will always exist. My hope is that we will never stop trying to know the creatures around us.

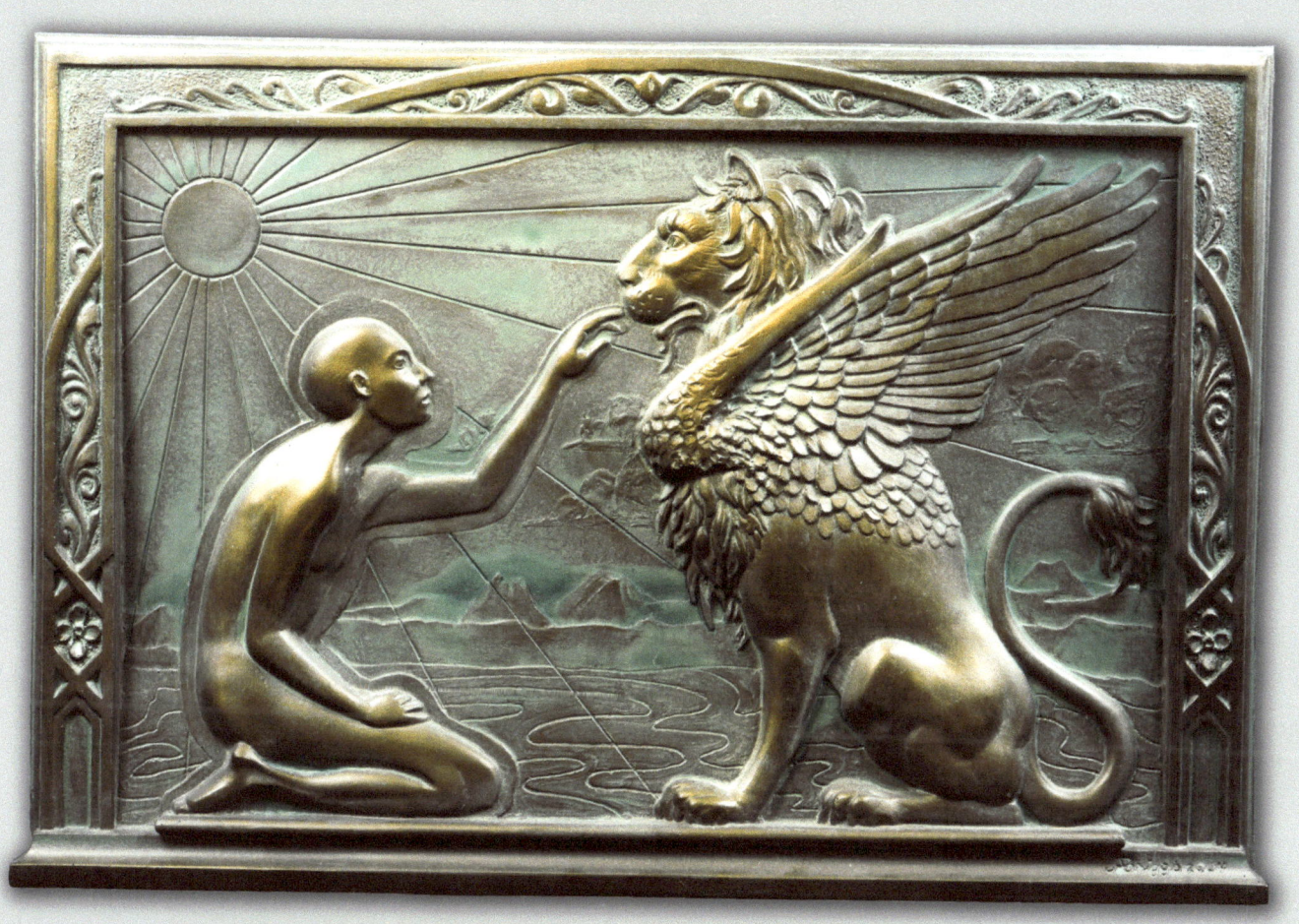

29

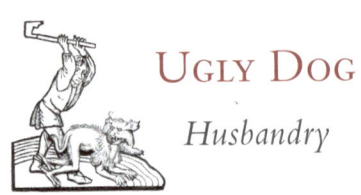

Ugly Dog
Husbandry

The World's Ugliest Dog Contest is an annual event held in Petaluma, California as part of the Sonoma-Marin Fair. The winner's owner receives a check for $1,600 and a trophy. There is significant media coverage. As many as 20,000–30,000 people attend the contest during the fair each year.

This is the 2011 winner –Yoda,– a previously abandoned, 14 year old, Chinese Crested-Chihuahua mix with a malformed nose, short tufts of hair, protruding tongue, and long hairless legs. Dog owners must provide documentation of veterinarian checks to determine the competing animal is healthy. Yoda died eight months after winning the contest.

The fair holds an all-day Dog Lover's Festival preceding the evening contest. In 2013, the contest celebrated its 25th anniversary. An anniversary book, THE WORLD'S UGLIEST DOG, was published containing pictures of Yoda's victory. The design for the Ugly Dog Relief was taken directly from one of these photos which includes the hands of the handler on the lower right and upper left.

When I first discovered this contest on the internet, I immediately thought of my grandfather's farm. In his breeding of animals, any newborn was carefully inspected for mutations. If a mutation was discovered, that animal was euthanized. This was to prevent a trait from migrating to a new generation. This practice is part of the breeding process called husbandry. Husbandry is management and conservation of resources; the care, cultivation, and breeding of crops and animals for their advancement. It seems strange to me that there would be a contest celebrating mutations.

Chimera, Teratoid and Monster have the same derivative meaning – a distortion of the natural order. There are grotesques in the corners of the frame warning against reckless husbandry.

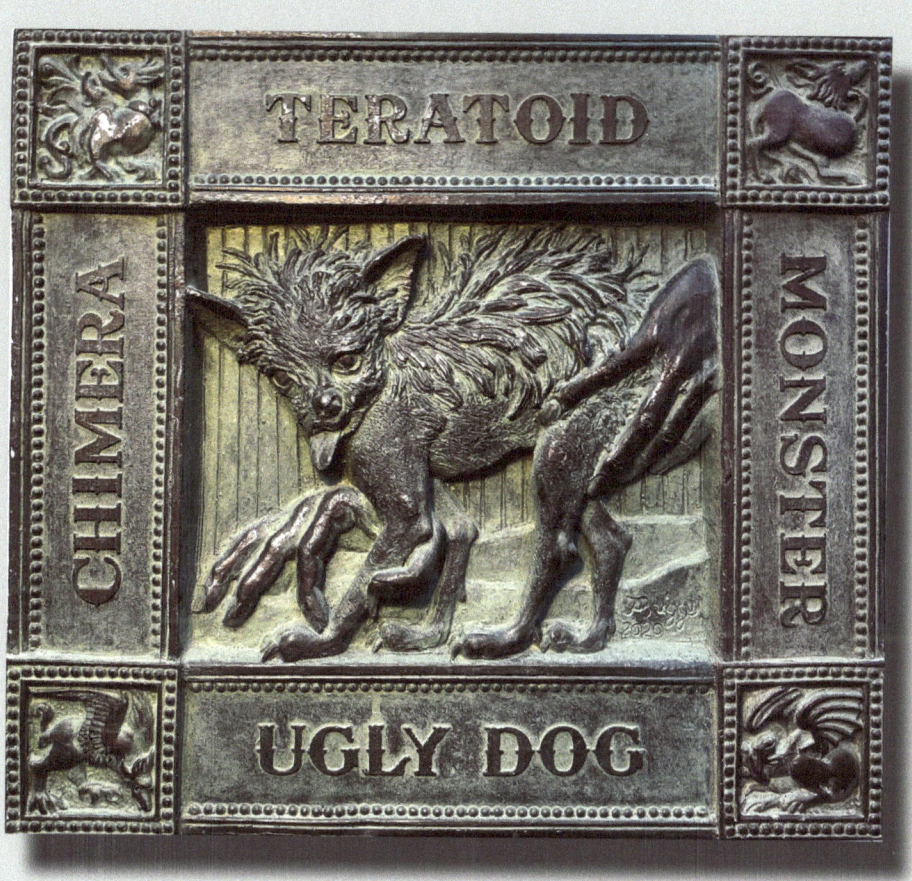

ANIMAL ALLEGORIES

Purchasing Information

All the reliefs shown in this book have been created using Forton MG, a polymer modified gypsum reinforced with fiberglass. It is used for sculpture because it is suitable for exterior use. It is also used on building facades. Each relief pictured has a faux bronze patina. Please e-mail Jeffrey for more information on any of the reliefs shown here or on his web site: **jeffrey@briggssculpture.com**

They are also available in cast bronze. Prices upon request.

Affinity
19.75" diameter x 1.25"

Babirusa
24.25" x 23.75" x 1.75"

Behemoth
24.25" x 23.75" x 1.75"

Demigod
24.25" x 18.5" x 2"

Hyena
28.5" x 22.5" x 1.75"

Kiwi
26.5" x 14.75" x 1.25"

Knossos
13.25" Diameter x 1.5"

Nereid
26.5" x 14.75" x 1.25"

Pegasus
31.5" x 22.5" x 2"

Predator
26.25" x 15.25" x 1.5"

Primordial Hunt
26.5" x 14.75" x 1.25"

Standard of Perfection
28" x 18.75" x 2"

Taxonomy
28.5" x 22" x 1.75"

The Messenger
28.5" x 18.75" x 1.5"

The Ugly Dog
13.5" x 21" x 2.5"

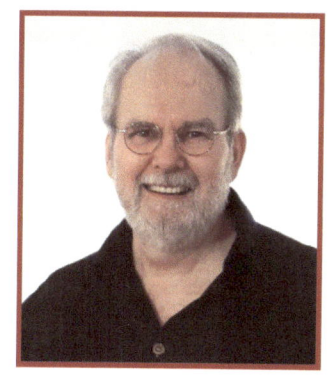

Jeff Briggs received his B.A. from Tufts University and his Diploma from Boston's School of the Museum of Fine Arts in 1969. His work has been featured in numerous national publications including *Yankee Magazine*, *Woodworking: The New Wave* by Donna Meilach, *Fine Woodworking Books* 11 and 111, and *Interior Design* to name a few. His art nouveau style sculptures were featured at *The Verbena Gallery* in New York and his wood sculptures are prized by collectors throughout the U.S.

He worked as sculptor and principle designer for *The Fabricon Carousel Company* for over 25 years, creating numerous Grand Carousels currently operating in Singapore, Finland, Saudi Arabia, Bolivia and throughout the USA. In 2006 the Detroit River Conservancy commissioned a carousel for it's revitalized riverfront park in downtown Detroit. Jeff piloted the design and sculpture of this 28 foot carousel with an unusual menagerie. Instead of traditional horses, the animals are all creatures indigenous to the Detroit River area including egrets, snails, loons, frogs, eagles, and herons.

Jeff's most recent project has been a custom carousel for the Rose Kennedy Greenway in Boston. Jeff designed and sculpted the entire carousel including all of the carousel creatures and scenery panels. Instead of the traditional animals, this carousel features rideable lobsters, cod fish, harbor seals and a host of other creatures from the land, sea and air that can be seen on or around the Boston Greenway. The carousel opened to the public in August of 2014.

When not making carousels Jeffrey creates sculpted wall reliefs. Thematically, the reliefs explore his thoughts about man's complex and paradoxical relationship to animals. His complete set of sculpted wall reliefs can be viewed at: **briggssculpture.com**

Briggs

jeffrey@briggssculpture.com

Other Books by Jeffrey Briggs

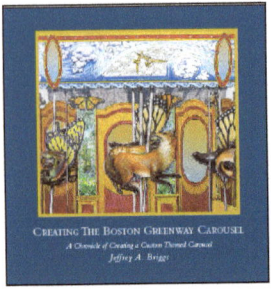

Creating The Greenway Carousel is a chronicle of how the Greenway Carousel in Boston, MA was created both conceptually and practically. The reader gets to experience both the creative and the decision making process, the science and technology, and the myriad of collaborations that it took to create this contemporary carousel. *Available on Amazon.com*

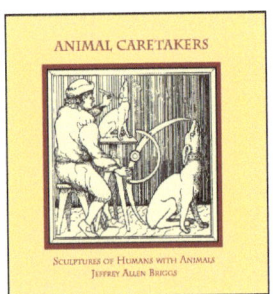

Animal Caretakers. The three-dimensional sculptures in this book illustrate the positive aspects of human impact on animals. Daily, farmers, animal breeders, veterinarians, and for that matter pet owners, are just a few categories of people who are advancing and protecting domesticated animals. The sculptures focus awareness on human psychological links to other animals. Our human need to nurture and protect, our need for companionship and love, are mixed with paradoxes of how we use and treat animals. *Available on Amazon.com*

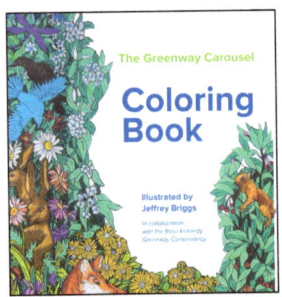

The Greenway Carousel Coloring Book is an adult coloring book of animal and decorative designs used to create the **Greenway Carousel.** As we entered the Anthropocene Age, increasing awareness of the animals that live on earth with us is crucial to the human stewardship of the earth. The carousel itself and this coloring book are part of this effort.

Available only through The Rose Kennedy Greenway.

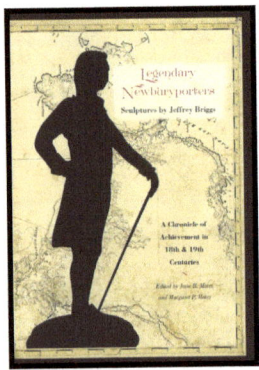

Legendary Newburyporters is an historian-written history of fourteen remarkable Newuryport individuals who contributed to the creation of the nation's democracy, industry, and economy. Each individual features photographs of Jeffrey's beautiful life-like sculptures. It is a chronicle of achievement in the 18th and 19th centuries when Newburyport, Massachusetts, was one of the primary centers of authority in our newly forming nation. *Available at the Custom House Maritime Museum, Jabberwocky Bookshop, in Newburyport, and on Amazon.com*

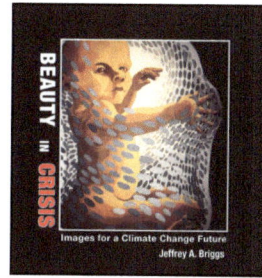

Beauty In Crisis is an attempt to create visual images of the environmental losses and future conditions that human habitation might look like.

"My emphasis is to learn about certain aspects of climate change and try to emphasize what those are, and create some kind of images. . . . .that can be used by those people in the trenches, fighting for us," he said.

To promote public use, Briggs said he's removed the copyright restrictions on all his images in the book. He said he wants to "just put it out there for them to be used. My aim is to help enhance the arguments for the things we have to do for climate change . . . to add an image to their efforts."

A picture is worth a thousand words," he said.

It's Briggs' fifth book and contains amazingly detailed drawings, paintings and portal-like images for a climate change future that began back in the 1970's.

Available on Amazon.com

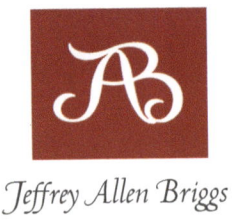

Jeffrey Allen Briggs

www.ingramcontent.com/pod-product-compliance
Lightning Source LLC
Chambersburg PA
CBHW050839180526
45159CB00004B/1962